Teach Them

Teach What Jesus Taught
Say what Jesus Said
&

Do what Jesus Did
To Make Disciples

Copyrighted Material

Contents

INTRODUCTION

In the process of making disciples, we introduce people to the faith. We expose them to the truths of our collective reality. We reveal our shortcomings, moral failures, ethical flaws, and spiritual blindness.

Then we show them a better way by introducing them to the "Way maker".

His name is Jesus Christ

He is our risen Savior

He leads us from the darkness

Into the marvelous light

INSTRUCTIONS

Disciple Makers,

Read through these lessons of the faith.

Discuss them with the ddisciples in your circle of influence. They may be other believers on your job, in your family, a part of your ministry, or they may be persons under your spiritual care. Implement these teachings in your ministry and help others I carry out the lessons in their lives.

Learn to say what Jesus said and do what Jesus did. Teach others what Jesus taught you. Teach them to obey the commands of Jesus.

Remember that Jesus will always be with you.

The Teachings

PREPARATION

Before Jesus' ministry began, John the Baptist went ahead of Him. John told the people to repent of their sins. He baptized them in the Jordan River as a sign of their confession of faith (in Jesus). John, representing the church, baptized with water, but Jesus would come to baptize them with the Holy Spirit.

The gospel writers recorded the ministry life of Jesus. We will follow the teachings of Mathew, the disciple who was a tax collector. As we follow Jesus' journey according to Matthew, your assignment is to prepare other disciples for their mission. Your job is to impart these teachings into them to help them carry out the work of the ministry. As you lead people to Jesus, you can also help them to grow in Christ.

1.Teach Disciples to Fish for people

Read Mark 1:16-20

Brief Background

Jesus was beginning His ministry. He was baptized in the Jordan River and driven by the Holy Spirit into the wilderness to be tempted. Jesus began preaching the good news. As He walked beside the Sea of Galilee, He chose some disciples and promised them that if they followed Jesus, He would teach them to "fish for people."

Read about our world today

Still today, Disciples of Jesus proclaim the truth of the gospel of Jesus Christ. We share the good news of His life, death, resurrection and second coming. We preach it, teach it, talk it, explain it, sing and shout it, dance to it, mime it, draw it, pray it and hope for it in everything we do.

Read Your Challenge

Teach disciples to share the good news. Find people who need to be impacted by the loving, saving, healing, whole person making ministry of Jesus Christ.

Discussion – What is the Good News (to you)?

_____

_____

_____

_____

What does the good news mean to someone who doesn't know Jesus Christ? What if they don't know that they need Jesus?

_____

_____

_____

_____

What is your difficulty when it comes to sharing the good news?

_____

_____

_____

_____

Read Matthew 9:9-12.

Jesus said that it is not the healthy that need a doctor, but the sick. Where are the spiritually sick? How can we share the good news with them?

_____

_____

_____

_____

What are some ways of approaching people with the gospel? How can you sense the right time (or opportunity) to share the gospel?

_____

_____

_____

_____

_____

Let's look at a few models

The confrontational approach:

Read about how Samuel challenged David in 2
Samuel 12:1-10 with the truth. He used a
confrontational approach that convicted David
of his sin.

The questioning approach:

Now, let's read how Jesus approached the
woman at the well in John 4:1-26. Jesus
outwitted her and forced her to face the truth.

The appeal to the human need:

Lastly, let's see how Jesus appealed to the
disciples' compassion for others when He sent
the disciples into the highways and bi-ways
(Matthew 22:1-14)

Discussion – Which method would you use?

_____

_____

_____

_____

When moved by God to share His gospel with others, what has worked for you?

_____

_____

_____

_____

2. Teach Disciples to Exercise Authority

Read Mark 1:21-28

Brief Background

God knows all things and God can do all things. Our Father gave Jesus His authority and ability to know and do all things too. Jesus demonstrated this by preaching and teaching. Then one day, Jesus showed His authority by healing a man and delivering him from an impure spirit.

There was a man in the synagogue who was possessed by an impure spirit. He cried out, "What do you want with us, Jesus of Nazareth". The impure spirit inside of the man knew that Jesus had authority. Jesus told the man to "Be quiet!" Then Jesus told the impure spirit to "Come out of him!"

This marked the beginning of Jesus' healing ministry. On that day, Jesus taught His disciples that He has all power and authority. By driving out impure spirits, Jesus proved that He can heal and deliver by the power of the Holy Spirit.

Read Your Challenge

Teach Disciples that Jesus has power and authority. Teach them that God's plan is to share His authority with His believers to accomplish His will on earth.

Discussion - What is Authority to you?

_____

_____

_____

_____

Read Daniel 7:13-14. Who is subject to Jesus' authority?

_____

_____

_____

_____

_____

Read Daniel 7:27. Who will inherit the kingdom and authority over the kingdom?

_____

_____

_____

_____

Do you believe that you have authority over all of creation, including the spirit world? If not, what will it take for you to believe?

_____

_____

_____

Notice how the Apostle Paul cast out the demon spirit in the slave girl in Acts 16:16-18? Why do you think Paul did this?

_____

_____

_____

_____

_____

In what ways would you exercise your spiritual authority? Would you use it to deliver others who are suffering from spiritual bondage?

_____

_____

_____

3. Teach Disciples to Care for people

Read Mark 1:29-31

Brief Background

At the home of Simon and Andrew, Simon's mother-in-law was in bed with a fever. Jesus took her hand and helped her up. Instantly, the fever left her and she began to wait on them. She served them out of gratitude for what Jesus had done for her.

Read about our world today

Jesus' miraculous healings teach the church that Jesus cares about everyone. This is true whether we are following Jesus on the road in ministry, or if we are at home spending time with our families.

Read Your Challenge

Teach Disciples to care for all people and to offer them the ministry of God's grace. Teach them to pursue the goodwill for all men. Teach them to encourage others to respond to Jesus' invitation and to live a life of humble service.

Discuss what it means to care for others

_____

_____

_____

_____

Read Psalm 8

Why does God care so much for us? Did we do anything to earn God's love?

_____

_____

_____

_____

The Disciples took Jesus to Peter's mother to help her. How can you connect a person in need with the healing power of God?

_____

_____

_____

_____

Read Psalm 44:1-10.

How should we respond to God when He heals us?

_____

_____

_____

_____

Read 3 John verses 1-4.

What areas of our lives does God care for?

_____

_____

_____

_____

_____

What spiritual needs are you able to meet for a
fellow Christian?

_____

_____

_____

_____

4.Teach that Ministry demands Sacrifice

Read Mark 1:32-34

Read the brief background

Later that evening when the people brought all the sick and demon-possessed to Jesus and the whole town gathered at the door, Jesus healed many who had various diseases. He continued to drive out the demons without allowing them to speak.

Read Our World

Jesus made time for people and He was teaching His disciples to do the same. Today, Jesus still teaches His disciples to welcome people, see their faces, hear their needs and act generously toward them. Disciples are most effective when we make ourselves, and our gifts available for ministry to others.

Read your challenge

God's power will improve the health and quality of life for all people. Teach Disciples

that God wants to transform us into whole,
healthy and grateful people. Teach them that
God alone has the power to do it.

Discuss the rejection and denial of Jesus

God did not permit the demons to speak
because even the demons knew who Jesus was.
If the demons knew who Jesus was, then why
do people still deny Him today?

_____

_____

_____

_____

Sometimes fear and pride prevents people from asking God for deliverance and healing. If God has given you power over demons, is it still possible to help them?

_____

_____

_____

_____

Is it possible to intentionally help those who are still hiding from Jesus in fear?

_____

_____

_____

_____

5. Teach Disciples to Pray before ministry

Read Mark 1:36-39

Read the Background

Jesus went away to pray in a solitary place early in the morning, while it was still dark. When the disciples found Jesus, he took them to the nearby villages to preach and heal because that is what He was destined to do!

Read about our world

Disciples need to experience the power and presence of God through fellowship with Him. Disciples will need it to operate in authority.

Read your challenge

Teach Disciples to seek solitude to pray, before starting the day. Teach them to commune with God before ministering to men and to spirits.

Define and discuss how Intercessory Prayer works

_____

_____

_____

_____

How important is it to find a place of solitude to pray each day?

_____

_____

_____

How do you enter into God's presence in your place of solitude?

_____

_____

_____

_____

_____

Read Job 42:7-8. What did God promise would happen if Job prayed for Eliphaz and his 2 friends?

_____

_____

_____

_____

Do you know the needs of the people that are closest to you in your life? What could you do for them?

_____

_____

_____

_____

_____

6. Teach that the Gospel cannot be hidden

Read Mark 1:40-45

Read the Background

A man with leprosy begged Jesus to make him clean if Jesus was willing. Jesus told the man "I am willing." Then He healed the man and told Him not to tell anyone. Instead, the man told everyone. People from everywhere came to see Jesus, causing Him to stay outside in a lonely place.

Read about our world

Our word is in a state of hopelessness. People need to know the good news that God sent His only son to us. Through Jesus, God is waiting for us. God is available and willing to meet our deepest needs. This good news cannot be hidden. It may seem that Jesus is hidden, but if you seek Him, He will be found. Disciples should always be willing to share the good news.

Read your challenge

Jesus taught the man that He is willing to heal the man if he needs healing and if he believes Jesus will do it. Teach Disciples that Jesus can and will do anything and everything. Men will seek out God when they realize they need God. Teach them to share the gospel to help others find Jesus.

Read Romans 1:16-17

Discuss how the gospel works. What does the good news reveal?

_____

_____

_____

_____

Read 1 Corinthians 15:1-2

What will the power of the gospel do if we hold onto it?

_____

_____

7.Teach disciples to have faith for others

Read Mark 2:1-5

Read the background

Four men dug through the roof of a crowded house in Capernaum. They lowered their friend, a paralytic man, to be healed by Jesus. Jesus forgave the man's sins and healed him because of his friends' faith.

Read about our world

Jesus proves that He honors faith, regardless of whose faith it is.

Read your challenge

Teach Disciples that their faith will move Jesus to perform miracles. Sometimes the miracles will benefit the disciples. Sometimes the miracles are for others. Disciples need faith at all times for all types of people and all types of results.

Discuss what it means to have faith for others.

_____

_____

_____

_____

Read John 11:14-15

Can your faith in God for someone else's need,

_____

_____

_____

_____

Read John 11:41-42

Can your faith for someone else truly move
God?

_____

_____

_____

_____

_____

Does it matter to God whose faith is activated when we direct our requests to Him?

_____

_____

_____

_____

Discuss Miracles

Read Exodus 10 about God's plagues against Pharaoh in Egypt. What moves God to do miracles?

_____

_____

_____

_____

Read Acts 2:14-21

Do you follow up with others to discuss the miraculous moves of God after they take place? Do you publicly affirm a move of God so unbelievers will acknowledge the power of God?

_____

_____

_____

_____

Develop a plan to help someone increase their faith

Identify one person that could use an increase in their faith. Draw closer to them. Find out what their needs are. Ask where their faith is and in regard to their needs. See if they are actively believing God to help them. Then help them connect their faith in God to do the impossible with their needs. This will help them increase their faith while you are believing for them.

_____

_____

_____

READ MARK 2:6-12

Brief Background

Jesus approached a lame man. Jesus could have told the man to get up and walk. Instead, Jesus operated from a greater level of authority by forgiving the man's sin.

Read about our world today

Jesus wanted to teach the unbelievers that as the son of God, He too was God. Jesus is teaching us that He too has the authority to forgive sins. Even today,

Read Your Challenge

Teach Disciples that Jesus has all of the authority. Only Jesus forgives sin. He forgives sin publicly and privately. He restores the sinner with life after they sin. He inspires the sinner to get up and live again. Jesus does all of this because Only He has the authority and the right to do so.

Discussion – What does it mean to have authority?

_____

_____

_____

_____

Read Colossians 2:9-10

Jesus Christ has authority over everything. He is calling you to live for Him fully. Is there anyone or any area of life where God does not have the authority?

_____

_____

_____

_____

Read Col 2:12

The world does not believe in Jesus, but you must follow the spirit, which leads to Jesus. You must believe in Him. You have a right to

_____

live for Jesus and a responsibility to live for Him.

What kind of character traits are you required to demonstrate?

_____

_____

_____

_____

Read Col 2:13

How should we treat others?

_____

_____

_____

_____

9.Teach inward devotion

READ MARK 2:18-22

Brief Background

Jesus taught that outward expressions of religion don't compare to internal devotion to God. Though some fast as a religious requirement, disciples must fast for a new heart. Their fast comes from a longing for God.

Read about our world today

Man needs an encounter with God to be renewed. An inward devotion to God helps prepare your heart for regeneration (a new life). A regenerated heart is like a new wine skin designed to hold a new batch of wine. It is like a cloth shrunken to perfectly fit and patch an old garment.

Read Your Challenge

Teach Disciples to prepare their hearts to become the temple of the Holy Spirit.

Discussion – What does it means to do devotions?

10.Teach Welcoming-ness

READ MARK 2:13-17

Brief Background

Jesus taught that it was ok to welcome unpopular people (e.g. tax collectors). It is ok to disciple people with a reputation for sinning, and people who believe in their own righteousness. They all need to be awakened.

Read about our world today

Today, Disciples need to know that everyone is sick with sin. We all need the forgiveness of God. We all need the healing and restorative power of God.

Read Your Challenge

Teach Disciples to be welcoming to sinners, especially the unpopular.

Discussion – What does it means to be welcoming?

_____

_____

_____

_____

_____

_____

_____

_____

_____

_____

_____

_____

_____

11. Teach that rules help us honor God

READ MARK 2:23-27

Brief Background

Jesus went into the synagogue on the Sabbath and healed a man with a shriveled hand. Jesus broke custom by healing on the Sabbath. It was the holy day where work was forbidden for the Jews.

Read about our world today

Jesus used this moment to teach that it was always ok to do good, even on a sacred day. Jesus created the Sabbath day for man to use to honor God.

Read Your Challenge

Teach Disciples that Jesus is the Creator of the Sabbath and the Lord over it. We set aside the Sabbath day to worship God together.

Teach Disciples that God made rules to help us honor God. God is worthy of the honor, so we should obey the rules. There is no rule or law; however, that should stop us from honoring God with our hearts. Nothing should stop us from worshipping God.

Discussion – What does it means to honor God?

_____

_____

_____

_____

_____

_____

_____

_____

_____

12. Teach that our lives are testimonies

READ MARK 3:7-12

Brief Background

Something unique happened when the crowds surrounded Jesus to be healed. The impure spirits would speak up. One day, they cried out that Jesus is "The Son of God." Jesus silenced the impure spirits. Then he gave strict orders not to tell anyone.

Read Your Challenge

Teach Disciples that when Jesus heals us, we are walking miracles. Our lives themselves testify just as much as the words from our mouths.

Define and discuss what it means to testify

13.Teach that division destroys

READ MARK 3:20-27

Brief Background

When Jesus drove demons out of people, the teachers of the law accused Jesus of being possessed by demons. Jesus taught them that their argument was illogical. He could not be both possessed by demons and able to cast out demons at the same time because that type of behavior would be divisive. Anything divided will be destroyed, whether it is a kingdom, house, or person.

Read Your Challenge

Teach Disciples that Jesus came to bind up the strong man (Satan) and put an end to his kingdom.

Teach Disciples to work together to wage spiritual warfare.

Define and discuss what it means to be divided
or united in spiritual warfare

_____

_____

_____

_____

_____

_____

_____

_____

_____

_____

_____

_____

14.Teach surrender to the Holy Spirit

READ MARK 3:28-30

Brief Background

When Jesus healed the people, Jesus was operating by the power of the Holy Spirit. This is the same spirit that would later raise Jesus from the dead.

Read about our world today

If anyone denies the Holy Spirit, they will commit the unpardonable sin. Denying the Holy Spirit would prevent them from receiving salvation and eternal life in Jesus Christ.

Read Your Challenge

Teach disciples that their life in Christ, and ministry in the church is fueled by the power of the Holy Spirit. There is no path to God except through His son, Jesus Christ, and there is no way to access His power except through the Holy Spirit.

Define and discuss what it means to surrender
to God

_____

_____

_____

_____

_____

_____

_____

_____

15.Teach that the church is a family

READ MARK 3:31-34

Brief Background

When Jesus was teaching, He ignored his mother and brothers, and said "Whoever does God's will is my brother and sister and mother". He was teaching that His church is a family.

Read about our world today

We disciples carry our crosses and die to ourselves (our old lives) daily.

Read Your Challenge

Teach disciples that in our new lives, we take on new identities, responsibilities, relationships, and gifts of God's grace.

Define and discuss what it means to be a part of the Christian family

16. Teach the Secret of the Kingdom

READ MARK 4:1-20

Read the Background

Jesus climbed aboard a boat and taught the crowd a parable about a man that sowed seed. The seed scattered on the path, on rocky places, among the thorns, and on good soil, but only the seed that fell on good soil produced a crop.

Jesus told the people this story about a farmer that was able to produce a good crop out of the ¼ of his seed. If there were any secret believers in the crowd, Jesus would have given them hope that something good would become of their lives. He taught the people that success is always possible.

Jesus talked to the disciples privately about the parable that He just shared publicly. He taught them that they were chosen to hear and truly understand the wisdom of God. Others will never understand the wisdom and teachings of God because they do not have the heart of God to understand Him. If they did,

His teachings would convict them and turn their hearts to God for forgiveness and repentance.

More importantly, Jesus taught the disciples one of the most important lessons, the secret of the kingdom. After sharing the parable with the crowd, and talking with the disciples privately about the parable, He went on to explain the mystery of the parable. He explained that Satan steals the word that lands on hardened hearts (like birds eating seed scattered on the path). Others less rooted in the word (e.g. on rocky places) face persecution and experience short lived joy. For some, the word is choked out by worries and desires; their hearts are thorny ground.

Jesus taught them the reality that spiritual warfare existed and took place on many fronts. Satan steals from us. Persecution attacks us. Our own worries and desires destroy us, but if we watch over and nurture our own hearts, we will be fruitful for the word that Jesus gives us.

Read about our world

Jesus' ultimate lesson is to expect great success, but it may only come from a small portion of the people. He taught the disciples to set realistic expectations. Everyone will not produce fruit based on the word we preach.

People will produce fruit if their hearts are good soil. If their hearts are ready, they will provide long lasting fruit from your ministry.

Read your challenge

Teach Disciples to prepare their hearts for what God is about to do through them!

Define and discuss the Kingdom of God

_____

_____

_____

_____

_____

_____

_____

_____

_____

_____

_____

_____

_____

_____

17. Teach Disciples to let their light shine

READ MARK 4:21-25

Brief Background

Jesus told his disciples that you don't hide a lamp under a bowl or bed. You put it on a stand. He was teaching them to stand up and be a witness, to share the gospel message with others, and to let their light shine before the world.

Jesus explained that whatever is hidden is meant to be disclosed and whatever is concealed is meant to be brought out in the open. This resembles the proverb that "It is the glory of God to conceal a matter; to search out a matter is the glory of kings." (Proverbs 25:2)

Read about our world today

Jesus taught the disciples that the precious treasures of God, whether they are a person, message, or spirit is to be shared, and treasured by man.

Read Your Challenge

Teach disciples to consider what they hear. If they use what they learn, they will get more. If they do not use it, it will be taken from them.

Define and discuss what it means to be a witness

_____

_____

_____

_____

_____

_____

_____

_____

_____

18.Teach that preaching grows the kingdom

READ MARK 4:26-29

Brief Background

Jesus taught a parable about the kingdom
of God. He said that a man scatters seed on the
ground that sprouts and grows by itself, night
and day. It produces but he does not know
how.

Read about our world today

Jesus is teaching the disciples to continue
to preach and teach and the kingdom will grow!

Read Your Challenge

Teach disciples that it is not their job to
produce the fruit. They do not need to know
how to make the kingdom grow. Their role is to
preach and teach. God will do the rest!

Define and discuss what it means to scatter seed

_____

_____

_____

_____

_____

_____

_____

_____

_____

_____

___

_____

_____

_____

_____

_____

19.Teach them to expect kingdom growth

READ MARK 4:30-34

Brief Background

Jesus used a parable to teach that the kingdom of God will grow like a mustard seed. It is the smallest seed but grows into one of the largest of all garden plants.

Read about our world today

Jesus is the mustard seed that will grow.

Read Your Challenge

Teach disciples that faith in Jesus Christ will add to kingdom growth. Disciples should expect to see the kingdom grow right before their eyes.

Define and discuss kingdom growth

_____

_____

_____

_____

_____

_____

_____

_____

_

_____

_____

_____

_____

_____

20.Teach Disciples to stay focused

READ MARK 4:35-41

Brief Background

When Jesus and the disciples were out on the boat, the disciples were afraid of the storm. Jesus rebuked the wind and the waves and asked His disciples why they were afraid. Then He asked if they still had any faith.

Read about our world today

Jesus taught them that He had authority over all of creation. When the storm came, He stayed focused. He used His faith to control the situation. He did not have fear. Instead he managed the distractions.

Read Your Challenge

Teach disciples to do the same: take authority, use faith, and manage the distractions while you are on the journey.

Define and discuss what it takes to stay focused

_____

_____

_____

_____

How do you know that something is a
distraction?

_____

_____

_____

_____

Read 2 Samuel 11:1-4

How do you turn away from a distraction?

_____

_____

_____

21.Teach them to learn when to go home

READ MARK 5:1-20

Brief Background

After Jesus healed the man name Legion, the man begged Jesus to let him go with Jesus. Jesus sent him home to his own people to tell them how much the Lord had done for him.

Read about our world today

Jesus was teaching that some people are called to follow Jesus, join the ministry and preach the gospel. Some are called to be living witnesses at home to their family, friends and neighbors.

Read Your Challenge

Teach disciples that we all have individual assignments. Sometimes we have to go home and share the good news.

Discuss what it means to have work, ministry and home life balance.

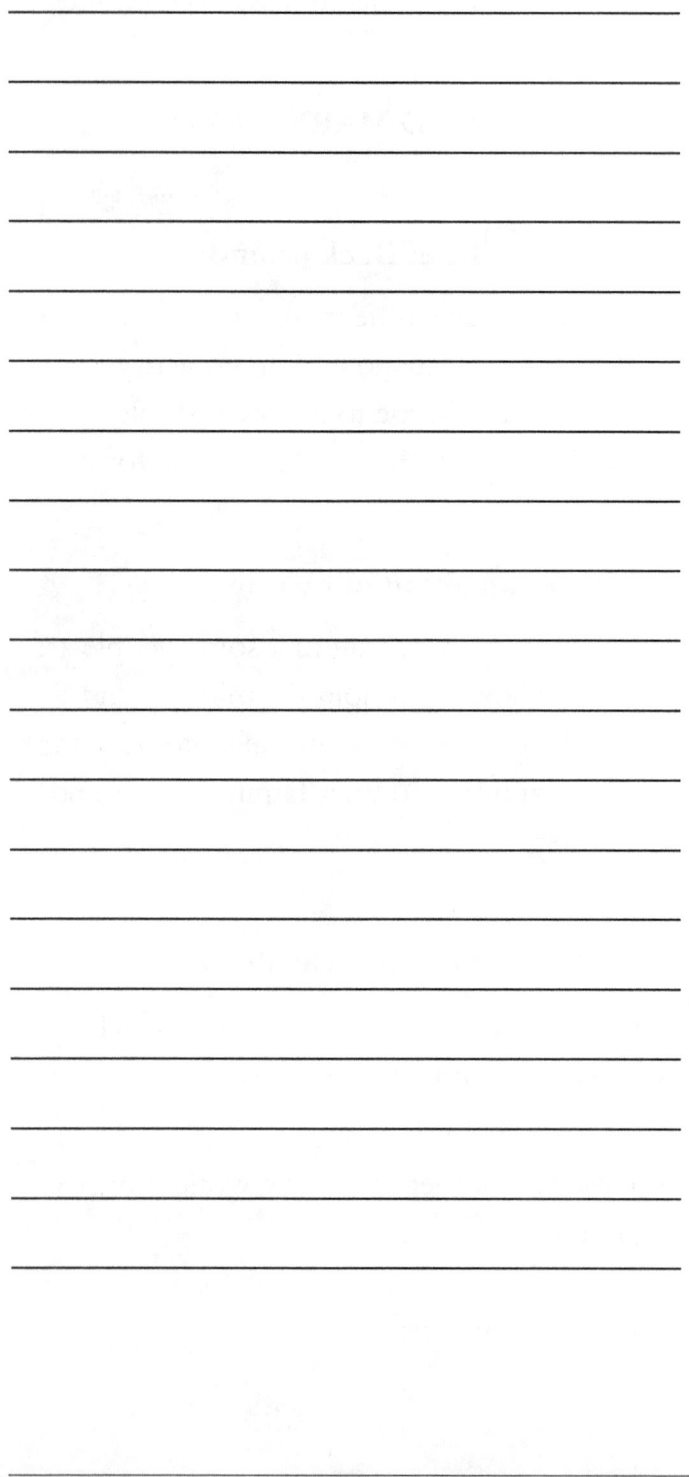

Teach Them!

Jesus gave the disciples the assurance that "these signs will accompany those who believe: In my name they will drive out demons; they will speak in new tongues; they will pick up snakes with their hands; and when they drink deadly poison, it will not hurt them at all; they will place their hands on sick people, and they will get well."

Teach disciples that power provides its own proof! If they believe, there will be miraculous signs and wonders in their day as there were in Jesus' day.

Closing

As we wrap up, remember that these 21 lessons are tools of transformation. You are not simply passing on information; you are shaping hearts, guiding souls, and building the Kingdom of God one life at a time.

Teaching what Jesus taught is your calling in Christ.

It is the sacred calling of every disciple-maker.

Go forth confidently. Walk with humility. Teach with authority. Love compassionately.

Teach them the word, everywhere, every day, in every way. Walk it, talk it, live it, and give all glory to God

I pray you bear the fruit of Christ, in Jesus' name, Amen.

Rev. Dr. Derrick L. Randolph, Sr.

On December 1, 2019, Dr. Randolph began his tenure as Pastor of the Christian Memorial Church in Baltimore, Maryland, la church founded on prayer and growing in the word of God. Pastor Randolph has inaugurated the Growing Together Ministry during the 2020 pandemic, with Virtual Worship and Prayer services, Discipleship classes, a media ministry with a thriving digital and Social Media presence. The church enjoys Leadership Gatherings, Men's Fellowship, and Marriage Ministry.

Dr. Randolph previously served as an Associate Minister at the New Psalmist Baptist Church, under the leadership of Bishop Walter Scott Thomas, Sr., where his ministry responsibilities included teaching small group Bible Study, Sunday school, Children's Discipleship and teaching Preparing for Marriage class.

Dr. Randolph earned a Master of Divinity Degree in 2010 at the Howard University School of Divinity and a Doctor of Ministry degree in 2015 at the United Theological Seminary in Dayton, Ohio under the Mentorship of Rev. Dr. William H. Curtis and Rev. Dr. Gina M. Stewart.

Dr. Randolph is also the founder of Journey of Faith Ministries, author of The Journey of Faith book series. He is a Christian Educator and author of several self-published books, including "The Word at Home", "Become – the Journey of Discipleship", "Becoming Me", and others. A bi-vocational pastor, Dr. Randolph maintains a career in management in federal government service. A former Baltimore City Public School teacher he is an advocate for raising the next generation.

Dr. Randolph wants to help equip God's people for works of service, so that the body of Christ may be built up and he is inspired to serve because "he who refreshes others will himself be refreshed (NIV)". Proverbs 11:25b

A native of Baltimore, MD, he is married to the former Ms. Sharon Renee Tabron. They are the proud parents of twin boys, Derrick Lamont Randolph Jr., and Joshua Isaiah Randolph.

Journey of Faith Ministries

www.ingramcontent.com/pod-product-compliance
Lightning Source LLC
Chambersburg PA
CBHW060349050426
42449CB00011B/2884

9 781944 166250